Book of DOG NAMES

Heroic Hounds

Literary Lapdogs

Faithful Fidos

Courageous Canines

& Precious Pooches

SIMON JEANS

 Sterling Publishing Co., Inc.   New York

Library of Congress Cataloging-in-Publication Data

Jeans, Simon.
    Book of dog names / Simon Jeans ; [illustrations by Sophie
    Blackall].
            p.   cm.
    Includes bibliographical references and index.
    ISBN 0-8069-8540-2
    1. Dogs—Names.   I. Title.
SF422.3.J43   1992
636.7'088'7—dc20   91-39284
                                                         CIP

Produced by The Watermark Press
Sydney, Australia
Design and Typesetting by Susie Stubbs
Cartoons reproduced by the kind permission
of The New Yorker Magazine, Inc.

10   9   8   7   6   5   4   3   2   1

First published in the United States in 1992
by Sterling Publishing Company, Inc.
387 Park Avenue South, New York, N.Y. 10016
Originally published in Australia and
© 1992 by The Watermark Press, Sydney, Australia
Additional drawings © 1992 by Sophie Blackall
Distributed in Canada by Sterling Publishing
% Canadian Manda Group, P.O. Box 920, Station U
Toronto, Ontario, Canada M8Z 5P9

Sterling ISBN 0-8069-8540-2

Introduction

What's in a name? More than most of us ever contemplate. Because a pet's name can be quirky, even eccentric, often more thought and research goes into the selection than that which is applied to the name of a child.

Here we provide examples from many sources, and information on previous bearers of the name. There's Bud who walked from Mexico to Kansas in the best Lassie tradition. And speaking of Lassie, her alter ego was Pal, a *laddie* who lived in luxury until he died at the age of nineteen.

In this small book are names of dogs both famous and obscure. Some are royal, many literary, a few cinematic, others democrat, some republican.

Included are suggestions for different breeds, different colors, different personalities. There are names for guard dogs, lap dogs, family dogs and working dogs. Whatever your taste, you are sure to find a name befitting your pampered pet; one that will be a credit to you, both when you shout it aloud in public places or say it more quietly at home.

"I started out carrying his newspaper and fetching his slippers. Then, gradually, I began assuming more and more responsibilities."

A

AARDVARK   Actually meaning "earth pig," an aardvark is a cross between an armadillo and an anteater. This would be a good, original name for an unusual looking, throwback sort of a dog.

AARON   Hank Aaron, one of baseball's immortals, or perhaps for the brother of Moses. Would suit a dog of noble deeds.

ABNER   After Al Capp's cartoon hero of (where else?) Dogpatch.

ACHILLES   Celebrated hero of Homer's epic *The Iliad*, known for his strength, energy and bravery. Heel, Achilles, heel!

ADAH   A good name for a female dog, as it means "ornament" in Hebrew. Insist on the "h" and give its pronunciation an aristocratic ring.

ADONIS   In classical Greek mythology Adonis was a beautiful youth, beloved of Aphrodite, killed by a boar while hunting. Not a name to take lightly.

AGLAIA　　This is the name of one of the three Graces, meaning "splendor," "beauty." It is rather doubtful whether you will ever meet another Aglaia, and you will enjoy explaining it.

AHENOBARBUS　　This was the surname of a Roman family, of which the emperor Nero was the last member. It actually means "yellow beard." A perfect name for the hound with a long, shaggy goatee and a cowardly streak. *See* NERO

ALARD　　Meaning "noble" and "hard," this is a name with lofty connections.

ALFRED　　Alfred means elf-counsel, elves being powerful nature spirits to the Anglo-Saxons. Or if your mutt has orange fur and a huge snout, then name him after the precocious alien furball in the TV series "Alf."

AMANDA　　From the Latin "amare," Amanda means "lovable." The diminutive Mandy is more commonly used for dogs.

AMBROSE　　From Greek mythology, meaning the fabled food and drink of the immortals, and hence the elixir of life. For the little pup who is the apple of your eye.

ANGUS   This good Scottish name comes from the Gaelic, meaning "unique choice," and has the very handy diminutive of Gus.

ANTONY   If your dog has changeable affections, name him after Marc Antony, who deserted his wife for the charms of Cleopatra.

ARCHIBALD   This name, which means "truly bold," has the short forms of Archie and Baldie. It brings to mind the famous "Archie" comics and their freckled, red-haired hero. A good name for an Irish Setter, perhaps.

ARGOS   Odysseus returned home in disguise after a twenty-year absence, as he still feared for his life. The only one who recognized him was his little dog, Argos, who died of joy when he saw his master.

ARTHUR   This popular name originates from Celtic words connected with "bear," and became popular due to the fame of King Arthur of the Round Table.

ASTA   The pet of Nick and Nora Charles, of the Thin Man films.

ASTERIX   A cult comic book hero, Goscinny and Uderzo's tiny Gaul lives in a village in northern France, and keeps the Romans at bay with the help of his dull-minded friend Obelix, and Getafix, the druid's magic potion. *See* DOGMATIX

ASTRO   The lazy but lovable dog in the space-age cartoon series, "The Jetsons." This name would suit larger breeds such as Great Danes or Irish Wolfhounds.

ATTILA   King of the Huns, called the "Scourge of God." Attila ravaged the Roman Empire before suffering his only defeat at Châlons-sur-Marne. For the dog who likes to mark his territory.

AUBREY   This is a good name for shorter breeds, deriving from the Old German name Alberic, king of the dwarfs. Oberon, the elfin king in Shakespeare's *A Midsummer Night's Dream*, is another name derived from Alberic.

B

BACCHUS   *see* DENIS, DENNIS

BAGEL   For a dog who enjoys a wholesome roll.

BAILEY   The dog who roams may be named for "Won't you come home?" Bill Bailey. The lazy soldier of cartoon fame also comes to mind.

BALOO   Rudyard Kipling's bear in *The Jungle Book*. For the mutt with a sweet tooth.

BALZAC   Honoré de Balzac, author of *La Comédie Humaine*, a work of over 50 volumes depicting aspects of contemporary society. For the dog who is a good judge of character.

BANDIT   Or Bandito, meaning a lawless desperado.
              For the outlaw dog who bites the postman
              and chases the milkman.

BARNABY   Barn and Barney are the short forms.
              Especially apt if your surname is Jones
              and your dog uses his nose to solve
              mysteries.

BARNUM   Phineas T. Barnum, of circus fame, is
              claimed to have said, "There's a sucker born
              every minute." For the dog who could be in
              the circus, or for that overly pampered
              pooch making a sucker of *you*.

BARRY   Barry was the name of a courageous St.
              Bernard who rescued at least 40 travellers
              lost in the snowy Alps between Switzerland
              and Italy at the turn of the 18th century.

BASIL   From the Greek, meaning "kingly." But
              if your pooch does not live up to such a
              regal moniker, just think instead of John
              Cleese's neurotic Basil Fawlty in "Fawlty
              Towers."

BEAUMONT   Ben Jonson wrote of fellow playwright
              Francis Beaumont, that "he loved too much
              himself and his own verse." So if your dog is
              an egotist, Beaumont would be ideal.

BEECHER   "The dog was created specially for children. He is the god of frolic." So wrote Henry Ward Beecher, in *Proverbs from Plymouth Pulpit* (1887).

BELL   There are so many derivations that we can only give a few. It may be an abbreviation of Isabel; or of Bellerophon, who attempted to fly to heaven on Pegasus; or of Bellona, the Roman goddess of war.

BELLE, BELLA   In French and Italian "lovely" and "beautiful," Bella is probably more commonly used than Belle.

BENEDICTINE   An order of monks who were renowned for their learning and played an influential part in the civilization of Europe. For the sober and serious hound.

BENJI   Benji, a modern shortening of the ancient Hebrew name Benjamin, "son of the right hand," is a very popular dog's name. Probably more so since the film *For the Love of Benji*.

BENSON   Recently a Papua New Guinean couple named their twin daughters Benson and Hedges. However, if you have only one mutt, remember there are several literary

Bensons in history, as well as the character from the TV series.

BEOWULF   This eighth-century poem from England tells of a courageous Geatish hero who defeats a hideous monster only to be ultimately slain by a dragon. Perfect for a vigilant guard dog.

BERNARD   The St. Bernard dog of Switzerland was named after St. Bernard of Menthon who founded the Alpine hospice for travellers. Some common short forms are Bernie, Barney and Nardie. *See* BARRY

BERTHA   A goddess of German ancestry, sometimes prefaced with Big. For the larger females.

BEVIS   In Sir Walter Scott's poem "Marmion," Bevis was the name of the red-roan charger. Bevis was also one of King Arthur's knights. It is a name suggesting chivalry and a shiny red coat.

BLACKIE   An affectionate family name, but highly unoriginal for a black pooch.

BLONDEL   According to popular legend, Blondel was a young troubadour who wandered Bohemia in search of Richard Lion-Heart, singing a

coded song until his imprisoned king re-
sponded. For the dog who howls when
there's a full moon.

BOATSWAIN   Byron was a great animal lover, and had
a small menagerie in his house in Italy,
including his enormous and much beloved
black Newfoundland Boatswain (pro-
nounced Bosun). The unfortunate dog died
of rabies.

BOGARDE/BOGART   Dirk or Humphrey. For the
dogs who talk tough but have a heart of gold
underneath.

BOND   James Bond, 007, the creation of Ian
Fleming. Would suit a suave male dog
popular with the ladies who likes his doggy
drinks shaken, not stirred. Grrrrr!

BONZO   A humorous dog created by George Studdy
in 1912. Bonzo enjoyed popularity for many
years; his image was reproduced on post-
cards, toys and in films. A lighthearted and
comical name.

BOO BOO   Yogi Bear's companion. For the little pup
who makes a few mistakes.

BOOGALOO   For that frolicsome, dancing dog.

BOOGIE   Boogie-woogie was a style of piano playing cultivated by early 20th-century jazz musicians. You and your canine would have to possess incredible talent or "Boogie Fever" to live up to this name.

BORIS   This name derives from a Russian word meaning "fight." For aggressive dogs of Russian descent.

BOSTON   For many years the cultural hub of American literary life and home to the social elite. Your hound would have to be an intellectual with impeccable social breeding.

BOSWELL   James Boswell, politician and author of *The Life of Samuel Johnson* (1791), was described after the discovery of his papers in the 1920s as "the best self-documented man in all history." For the dog who faithfully takes note of everything.

BOUNCE   The poet Alexander Pope, who was very frail and seriously handicapped, had a protector in his Great Dane, Bounce. The huge hound actually saved Pope from an attack by a corrupt servant.

BOUNDER   For that irrepressible cur that cuts a great caper.

BOWSER   Derived from "drunkard," this would suit a
           lively dog who likes a regular bottle of milk.

BOY   The earliest Poodle heard of in Britain, Boy
           was given to Prince Rupert of the royal
           Stuarts during his imprisonment at Linz in
           1640. The pooch was feared by Cromwellian
           soldiers, who thought he was a dog-witch
           with the gift of languages and prophesy.

BRAG   There is an old saying, "Brag is a good dog,
           but Holdfast is better," which means that
           doing something is better than just talking
           about it. Shakespeare alludes to it in *Henry
           V:*

"Trust none;
For oaths are straws, men's faiths are wafer cakes, And holdfast is the only dog my duck."
So Brag for a dog who barks but never bites?

BRAN   The dog of Fingal, the legendary Irish hero, was a great favorite and is mentioned in Scott's *Waverley:* "If not Bran then it is Bran's brother" (in every way as good).

BRUCE   Deriving no doubt from the 13th-century hero, Robert the Bruce. The name is of Norman origin and Brewis is one of its forms. It used to be enormously popular, but nowadays the name is considered a tad ordinary.

BRUNO   Traditionally, this is a name for a brown dog. It was the name of an early Archbishop and a saintly Carthusian, and was probably developed from the Old German "brun," where the surname Brown and the term brunette came from.

BRUTUS   This Roman suffered agonies of mind when he became embroiled in the plot to stab Julius Caesar to death. For the hound who brings his daggers out when your back is turned.

BUCK   In its archaic form this could mean "my dear fellow" or it could be the name of a fop or a dandy. It also brings to mind the hero from the TV series "Buck Rogers in the 25th Century."

BUD   In the tradition of *Lassie Come Home*, a collie named Bud travelled 800 miles to rejoin his departed American owners when they moved. A good name for a faithful dog.

BUMBLE   Reminiscent of the bee, and so a perfect name for a barrel-shaped brindle dog. Also the name of the beadle in Dickens's *Oliver Twist*, who brings us the term "bumble-dom," meaning foolish officiousness.

BUMMER   If your pooch scrounges through garbage, or if he's just footloose, here's a good name.

BURGER   If the implications of this take-out name do not appeal, name your dog after 18th-century poet Gottfried August Bürger (1747-1794) or the U.S. Supreme Court Chief Justice of the same name.

BUSTER   A vulgar form of "burster," implying an abundance of vitality, or something that takes one's breath away. Also an affectionate term akin to "buddy."

BUTCH Outlaws Butch Cassidy and the Sundance Kid occupy a favorable place in popular history, due mainly to the Hollywood film starring Paul Newman and Robert Redford.

BUTTONS Bright as a button; well suited to a lively and playful pup. Or a dog that's red in color, after Red Buttons, the comedian.

C

CAESAR A Wire-Haired Terrier named Caesar was the last and best-loved dog of King Edward VII. He once bit the seat of the then Prime Minister, Herbert Asquith, who sat in the mutt's chair by mistake. The titles Kaiser, Czar and Tsar are variants of the name.

CAMP Sir Walter Scott's devotion to dogs is evident in his books. Camp was a crossbreed, part Bulldog, part Rat-Terrier.

CAMPBELL The name of a noble Scottish clan. This would be a perfect name for a West Highland White or a Scottish Terrier.

CANDY   A sweet name. No need to worry about this dog's bite; its teeth should be completely rotten.

CAPER   For the bouncy hound who likes to jump about.

CAPULET   A noble name, taken from one of the feuding families in Shakespeare's *Romeo and Juliet*. Juliet came from the Capulets and Romeo from the Montagues. If your pooch is having an ongoing conflict with a dog down the road, then this would fill the bill.

CASEY   Name your dog after Casey Stengel, and you may end up with a dog of questionable oratorical abilities.

CASSIDY   *see* BUTCH

CATO   This spaniel was a gift from Henry VII to his ambassador Lord Wiltshire, who took him on a diplomatic visit to the Pope in Rome. In an age-old gesture the Pope extended his toe to the Lord, but Cato misunderstood, bit the papal toe and was hacked to death by the papal guards.

CAVALL   King Arthur of Round Table fame's favorite dog.

CERBERUS *see* PLUTO

CHARLES Names of three Merovingian kings of France will amuse: Charles the Bald (823-877), Charles the Fat (839-888) and Charles the Simple (879-929). Take your choice.

CHARLEY Author John Steinbeck travelled America with his dog Charley, and later wrote a book about their adventures, appropriately titled *Travels with Charley*.

CHECKERS Richard Nixon's dog, and the subject of the famous "Checkers" speech of the early 1950s. A great name for a dog whose loyalty

doesn't demand anything more than a good Pat.

CHESTER   A historic town in Britain where some of the Mystery Plays were performed; but today the name recalls sideshow images of clowns in checked trousers, bright wigs and red noses.

CHINOOK   A warm wind blowing down the eastern slopes of the Rocky Mountains. A beautiful name.

CHIP   One half of the chipmunk duo Chip and Dale, from the Walt Disney cartoon. Ideal for a small, mischievous dog.

CHUCK   An all-American name. If you catch your dog singing into his bone in front of the mirror, it   could lead to a musical career like that of Chuck Berry.

CICERO   From the Latin word "cicer," meaning wart. Marcus Tullius, the great Roman statesman, was called Cicero because he had a small growth on the top of his nose. May be abbreviated to Cissy.

CLAUDE   Comes from a clan name probably meaning "limping." When Claudius became Roman emperor, many flattered him by asserting his name came from a word meaning "glorious." For the dog who hears only what it wants to hear.

CLINT   From Clint "Go ahead, make my day" Eastwood.

COCO   Choose this name for a dog, and it may live up to Chanel's reputation for simple, yet elegant, lines.

COLIN   Colin, though it may not sound like it, is the perfect name for a dog. It derives from the Celtic word "cailean" which means "a young hound." It is possible that the name Collie also derives from this word.

COLONEL   A name used in *101 Dalmatians*, by Dodie Smith. Other regimental titles can also be suitable for the right character. *See* MAJOR

CONRAD   Sometimes used for a roving dog, but it is also apt for an analytical dog, following in the footsteps of the writer Joseph Conrad (1857-1924).

CUPID   Charles II was a great dog lover (King Charles Spaniels are named for him). The first spaniel he owned was given to him after his coronation and was named Cupid. For the dog who steals your heart.

D

DAISY — This name actually derives from the Anglo-Saxon "day's eye" because the daisy closes its petals as night approaches. For the pooch who appears "fresh as a daisy" in the morning.

DANDY — Meanings span from the Dandie Dinmont breed of terriers to an elegantly dressed fop.

DANNY — The abbreviated form of the biblical name Daniel also has associations with Irish folk music ("Oh Danny Boy") and movie star (Danny Kaye). For the multitalented mutt.

DANTE — The name itself is an abbreviation of Durante, which comes from the Latin "lasting," and if Durante recalls to older people the comedian Jimmy, this might be a good name for a dog with a prominent nose.

DARWIN   What more inspiring name could you give to a dog than that of Charles Darwin, the man who gave us the modern theory of evolution? To paraphrase Darwin, it's survival of the fittest in this dog-eat-dog world.

DASH   In Pidgin English, dash can mean a free gift, so if your family pet was given to you as a present, then this could fit. It is also a euphemism for "damn," used in the 19th century as an inoffensive swear word.

DAVE   A common nickname, and great for that common mutt, your old friend and companion. As a shortening of David, it may suit the small dog who stands up to neighborhood Goliaths.

DEIMOS   The planet Mars has two satellites, Deimos and Phobos, words from the Greek meaning "panic" and "terror." They are very close to the planet and difficult to observe from Earth. Appropriate for an inseparable duo or trio.

DELILAH   That beautiful but treacherous woman of "Samson and Delilah" fame (*Judges* XVI). *See* SAMSON

DENIS, DENNIS   This name derives from the Greek Dionysos, better known as Bacchus. Dennis is the Irish version, and the name of a popular comic character, Dennis the Menace, who lives up to his name. For the mischievous pup who digs up your roses or chews your slippers.

DEVIL   For your own little devil, either a large fierce looking dog, or ironically, a small, harmless terrier, or name him after the faithful dog who belongs to the Phantom of comic strip fame, the ghost who walks.

DIAMOND   Diamond, the little dog of Sir Isaac Newton, the famous 17th-century scientist and astronomer, once set fire to records of experiments Newton was working on by accidentally knocking over a candle. For the clumsy but lovable mutt.

DIGGORY   From the French "égaré," "strayed" or "lost," this is a very good name should your dog happen to be a foundling. Also, Thomas Hardy used it for a character in *The Return of the Native* (Diggory Venn), C.S. Lewis named one of the children in the Narnia Chronicles Diggory and it was also the name of the rustic serving man in *She Stoops to Conquer*, by Goldsmith.

DINO   For the dog that bowls you over when you walk in the door and then eagerly licks your face. All you can say is "Down, boy," as does Fred Flintstone in the TV cartoon "The Flintstones."

DISNEY   Walt Disney (1901-1966), the great cartoon film producer and creator of Mickey Mouse, Donald Duck, et al.

DOBIE   An obvious name for a Doberman Pinscher. That perpetually perplexed teenager, Dobie Gillis of TV fame, also comes to mind.

DOG   When nothing else seems to fit. And as Aldous Huxley pointed out in *Antic Hay*, it spells "God" backwards.

DOGMATIX   Asterix's small, white, Gaulish dog from the Asterix comic strip series. *See* ASTERIX, OBELIX

DOLLAR   For the dog that increases in value.

DOMINI CANES   Literally, "Hounds of the Lord," this name was applied to the order founded by the Spaniard St. Dominic. To make it easier to call out, it can be abbreviated to Dom.

DOMINO An ideal name for a Dalmatian, or in praise of Fats Domino, the musician.

DOOKIE *see* WINDSOR

DOROTHY Dorothy derives from the Greek words "doron," meaning "gift," and "Theou," meaning "of God." Also brings to mind Dorothy from the classic *The Wizard of Oz*. Shortenings include Dot, Dottie, Dodo, Dodie and Dora.

DUCHESS Like Princess, Prince, King and Queenie, this is a highly unoriginal name, but small children love it.

DUDLEY One of a number of illustrious surnames, most belonging to ancient, noble families. Gradually they have come into use as first names.

DUKE Derived from, "dux," meaning "leader" in Latin, whence came the title "Il Duce," for Benito Mussolini, the Italian fascist dictator. It was also Hollywood Western star John Wayne's nickname, which he took from a childhood pet.

DYLAN Either for Bob Dylan or Dylan Thomas. If your pup seems to be a budding poet or sings a bit off-key, this may be the perfect name.

E

E.T.   Steven Spielberg's immortal character E.T. was not the most handsome of creatures, so bear that in mind when you name that odd-looking beast who arrived on your doorstep, seemingly out of nowhere.

EDITH   Edith Bunker, long-suffering wife of Archie, and America's best-loved dingbat. A great name for a dog who'll put up with his master's worst behavior and still find love in his heart.

EINSTEIN   Possibly a good name for a slow starter. Albert Einstein's parents feared he was backward during his early school years. Then in 1916 he produced a general theory of relativity.

ELMER   Although its origins come from the Anglo-Saxon "Aethelmaer" ("noble famous") the name is now associated more with American fictional characters like Elmer Gantry and Elmer Fudd, the farmer with the speech impediment and an aversion to wabbits.

ELSA   Most famous as the lioness in the book *Born Free*, Elsa could also apply to dogs of the more leonine breeds such as Collies or German Shepherds.

ELVIS   Presley, the King. A perfect name for a hound dog.

ENGELS   The German political figure Friedrich Engels wrote *The Condition of the Working Class in England* in 1844, co-wrote *The Communist Manifesto* with Marx in 1848 and completed *Das Kapital* in 1894 after Marx died. Strictly for the working-class mutt.

ERASMUS   Desiderius Erasmus (c. 1466-1536), the Dutch Renaissance theologian and scholar.

ERIN   An ancient and poetic name for Ireland, perfect for an Irish Wolfhound.

ERNEST   The importance of being earnest — this name means what it says. Short forms are Ern and Ernie. Think of naming a pair Bert and Ernie, after the quarrelsome duo in "Sesame Street."

ERROL   Hollywood's great swashbuckler and "charming rogue" of the late 1930s and early 1940s, Errol Flynn starred in such films as *Captain Blood*, and *The Adventures of Robin Hood*. Only for a dog who steals bones from the rich to give to the poor.

EREBUS   In Greek mythology, Erebus was the son of Chaos and the brother of Night. Darkness personified. For the coal-black dog.

ETHEL   Ethel Merman, Broadway star. If your pet's bark needs no amplification, here's a name for her.

F

FAITH   A fine name for the dog who was sold to you as a pedigreed pooch, but somehow the breeder just couldn't find the registration papers. It also suggests the loyalty and faithfulness of man's best friend.

FARAMUND   Although of German origin, this name
was brought to England by the Normans. It
is a compound of "fara," meaning journey,
and "mund," meaning protection. Good for
a traveller's dog.

FARFEL   The Dachshund puppet from the 1950s
Nestlé hot-chocolate commercials. For the
dog who can spell, albeit with a New York
accent.

FARQUHAR   The name of an early 18th-century Irish
playwright.

FATTY   One of the puppies in *101 Dalmatians* by
Dodie Smith. Also brings to mind Fatty
Arbuckle and Fats Domino.

FELIX   Although from the legendary cartoon cat of
the same name, it can still be applied to a
cheerful, friendly dog, as Felix means "hap-
piness."

FERDINAND   Same derivation as FARAMUND. For
the adventurous dog who has maybe
watched *Lassie Come Home* one too many
times.

FERGUS   "Manly choice," or "supreme choice," it was
a popular name for Celtic saints. Fergus is

still common in Scotland, as is the surname Ferguson. And, for the royalists, Fergie is a short form. Gus would be stretching it.

FIDO This name comes from the Latin "fidelio" meaning "the faithful one." It has become *the* generic dog name.

FIFI The shortened form of Fiona should only be used for that very small, very pampered French poodle.

FIORELLO Name your dog for the once mayor of New York, and you might find that he loves reading the Sunday comics to the kids — or maybe using them some other way (and the sports section too!).

FLOSS This is, of course, an abbreviation of Florence, rarely used before the fame of Florence Nightingale, the "Lady with the Lamp," gave it fresh impetus. It is a homely name that needs no apology.

FLUSH Elizabeth Barrett's Spaniel, Flush, was nearly destroyed by the poet's father after her romantic elopement with Robert Browning. Her sister and a servant managed to sneak Flush out of the home, and he lived with Barrett to the end of his days.

FRANCO   This Spanish dictator was not renowned for his policies on human rights, so your dog might use this name as a cue for antisocial behavior.

FRANKLIN   A dog named Franklin is the perfect companion when flying a kite in a thunderstorm — which, of course, was how Benjamin Franklin discovered electricity.

FRANZ   A dog can sometimes feel he is in an enigmatic and callous world, riddled with guilt and loneliness, where the ordinary often becomes sinister. The Czech novelist Franz Kafka wrote about such feelings, so let your dog know he's not alone out there.

FRECKLES   Ideal for a dog with a pied or ticked coat, perhaps a Dalmatian or a German Shorthaired Pointer.

FRED   Is your dog as light on his feet as Fred Astaire or companion to another pet named Ginger? Either way, this is a simple and pleasant name.

FREDDY/FREDDIE   Freddy is actually an old German compound of "frithu," which means "peace," and "ric," which means "ruler." If your hound has unusually long claws, name him after *Nightmare on Elm Street* baddie Freddie Krueger.

FRITZ   Would suit a Germanic breed, in particular the Dachshund.

FRODO   Noted character from J.R.R. Tolkien's magical fantasy novels. A wonderful name for a woodsy type of dog with a sense of humor.

FUNGUS   Raymond Briggs's *Fungus the Bogeyman* is a picture book which has enjoyed cult status. The subterranean life-style of the Bogeys

and their dislike of the "Dry Cleaners" or humans has repelled and delighted adults and children alike.

G

GABLE   *see* KING

GALILEO   Galileo Galilei (1564-1642), the Italian astronomer, established the scientific testing of theories and was among the first to use a telescope for astronomy. Only for the star-struck dog.

GARNET   For a precious dog, as garnet is a jewel.

GAUDY   From the Latin "gaudium," meaning joy.

GELERT   This is the name of the dog that Llewellyn, a Welsh prince, received in dowry from his father-in-law, King John. Llewellyn killed him after mistakenly thinking some blood found on his baby was due to an attack from the dog. Instead Gelert had actually saved the child from being killed by a wolf.

GENGIST   Gengist was a giant hound owned by
              Frederick the Great of Prussia. During
              Prussia's war against the Russians, Gengist
              saved Frederick's life during a Cossack raid
              by making him hide behind a bush.

GEORGE   Virgil called his poems on farming the
              Georgics because George actually means
              "tiller of the ground." The most famous
              George was St. George, who killed a
              dragon. His day is April 23rd. *See* VIRGIL

GERONIMO   The Chiricahua Apache chief (1829-
              1909). "Geronimo!" is also well known as
              the cry uttered before parachuting out of a
              plane. For the dog with a head for heights.

GERTRUDE   The original Gertrude was one of the
              Valkyries, the maidens in Norse mythology
              who took those heroes killed on the battle-
              field to the palace of bliss, Valhalla. The
              name actually means "spear-strength."

GINGER   From Middle English "gingivere," this name
              denotes a redhead. Or after the Hollywood
              actress Ginger Rogers. A red Silky Terrier,
              perhaps.

GODZILLA   The name that applies to that ferocious
              screen monster, twice as big as the tallest

skyscraper, could be quirkily applied to a little canine with a big bark.

GOETHE   Johann Wolfgang von Goethe wrote, "Wanted: a dog that neither barks nor bites, eats broken glass and shits diamonds."

GOLDIE   Along with Wolf and Prince, Goldie was one of Hitler's German Shepherd dogs. Still, a pleasant enough name.

GOOFY   The name of this popular Disney dog, a friend of Mickey Mouse, has become synonymous with clumsiness.

GORBY   A diminutive of Gorbachev, which many would regard as ideologically sound. You may also consider "Perestroika" or "Glasnost" as pet names of our time.

GRENVILLE   *see* DUDLEY

GRIEG   The name of Paul Newman's dog. Grieg, the Norwegian composer, is one of Newman's favorites.

GROUCHO   One of the three Marx brothers, along with Harpo and Chico. The team originally included brothers Gummo and Zeppo. All extremely becoming dog names.

GROWLY   A puppy in *101 Dalmatians*, who aspired to be fierce.

GUINNESS Stout made by the firm of Guinness from Dublin. It is a rich and creamy black beer and so could refer to a dog of similar coloring.

GYPSY   Charles Dickens, himself a dog lover, introduced several dogs into his novels. A memorable one was the little spaniel Gypsy, always called Jip, who belonged to Dora, David Copperfield's "child bride."

H

HAMLET   The only name for a mutt that has problems making up his mind or is overly fond of his mother. More archaic forms of the name are Amlet and Ambleth.

HAPPY   The name of George V's royal dog. Also the name of one of the dwarfs in the 1937 Walt Disney cartoon *Snow White and the Seven Dwarfs*, appropriate if your pet is pint-sized.

HARDY and LAUREL   The manic slapstick comedy duo.

HARPO   Marx, the quiet one. *See* GROUCHO

HARRY   Harry is a diminutive of Henry, which came about in an effort to imitate the French pronunciation, Henri. Hank is another, American version.

HEATHCLIFF   The dark, powerful hero of Emily Brontë's *Wuthering Heights*. Always associated with darkness, it might suit a black dog. An impressive and potent name.

HECTOR   The hero of Troy, slain by Achilles. A good name for the mean-looking dog always ready for a good fight.

HELEN   The Trojan War was her fault. Name your dog for this seductress, and you might find an invasion force at your doorstep.

HERALD   This, together with Heral, Herolt and several others, was an 11th-century version of Harold. This could be the perfect name for the mutt who likes to fetch his owner's newspaper in the morning.

HOLDFAST *see* BRAG

HOMER The Greek epic poet. A fine name for the dog of heroic adventures. Or a name for the athletic dog who can round all the bases.

HONEY For the lovable light-colored dog.

HORATIO The faithful companion of Hamlet makes a delightful name for a canine friend.

HOSANNA We are more likely to hear this as an exclamation at a revivalist meeting than to find that a friend has chosen it as a name for a dog. Still, a joyous name that deserves resurrection.

HOTEI This is a Japanese name that is easy to pronounce. In Japanese folklore, there were seven gods of luck, of which Hotei was the god of joviality.

HOTSPUR Shakespeare's Hotspur's real name was Sir Henry Percy, but he was better known as Harry Hotspur, a name which probably came from the impetuousness of his attacks.

HOWARD Howard Hughes, the fabulously rich recluse, or Howard Cosell, the mellifluous sports commentator. A fine name for the dog who loves his little corner and won't leave it, or for the long-winded dog. *See* DUDLEY

HUCKLEBERRY   A rather cumbersome but charming
name for an adventurous young dog. Easily
shortened to Huck.

HUGO   Victor Hugo (1802-1885), author and
politician, apostle of Romanticism,
libertarian, humanitarian, and democratic
idealist, who wrote *Les Misérables.* For
an old and intelligent breed.

HUMPHREY   There are several versions of this
name, which was widely used in the Middle
Ages. The original form was Humfrey. The
nursery hero Humpty-Dumpty was no doubt
originally called Humfrey.

HYDE   For the dog who has a good and a bad side.
See JEKYLL

I

IKE   Dwight David Eisenhower, World War II
general and later President of the United
States (1953-1961). Name your dog Ike
and you may find him roaming the golf

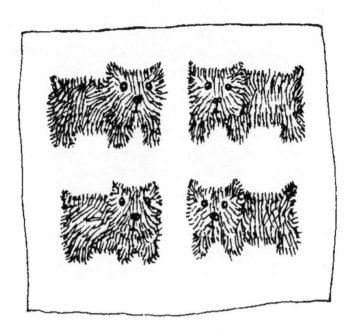

course instead of tending to important matters.

IRVING   Washington Irving, the famous novelist, wrote about life in 18th-century New York. A fine name for the dog who prefers to find a humorous side to history.

ISENGRIN   *See* REYNARD

IT GIRL   The name given to U.S. film star Clara Bow, the sex goddess of Hollywood in the Roaring Twenties, reputed to have made love to an entire football team.

IVAN   The Russian version of the name John. Ivan the Terrible, the first tsar of Russia, was a man of great cruelty. "Ivan Ivanovitch" is used to denote the national personification of Russia, like the English "John Bull."

IVES   Charles Ives, the American avant-garde composer. If his bark's a bit atonal this is the right name.

IVOR   From a Welsh word meaning "lord." For the canine with royal lineage.

J

JACK   The Scottish is Jock. Jack is a nickname for John, it became very common during the 14th century—hence, its wide use in nursery rhymes. There is Jack Horner, Jack and the Beanstalk, Jack and Jill, to name just a few.

JACKIE   A great name for a Bouvier des Flandres.

JACKSON   Some prominent Americans in this list include: Andrew Jackson, America's seventh

President; Thomas "Stonewall" Jackson, a Confederate general; and the most famous of all, Michael Jackson. For the reclusive pet.

JAGGER   Name your dog after Mick Jagger if he's a rocker with great staying power.

JAKE   An American alternative to Jack or Jacques, which are nicknames for John.

JASON   Of Golden Fleece fame.

JED   For the simple country dog who finds the high life a bit of a joke, as in Jed of "The Beverly Hillbillies."

JEFFERSON   Thomas, President of the United States 1801-1809. Especially apt if your dog likes air travel.

JEKYLL   Half of Robert Louis Stevenson's classic tale *The Strange Case of Dr. Jekyll and Mr Hyde*, published in 1886.

JEMIMA   This is the name of the rebellious little girl who, when she was good, could be very, very good, but when she was bad, she was horrid. The name actually means "dove," and she was one of the daughters of Job.

"He's about five feet six, has big brown eyes and curly blond hair, and answers to the name of Master."

JENNY   An attractive and domestic name, which Dante Gabriel Rossetti used as the basis for his poem about a beautiful and flaxen-haired prostitute.

JESS   A very popular name for a farm dog, male or female. In both cases it is an abbreviation. It is a pet name for any male dog called Jesse, Jessop (a form of Joseph) or Joshua. It is also a shortening of Jessica, which means "God is looking," and Jessie.

JESTER   Why not give the cheerful clown in your house this name?

JET   Denoting a deep glossy black dog, this name would suit a Labrador.

JETHRO   Nephew of Jed Clampett. A good name for a dog who's got a great build, but who's still something of a yokel.

JOCK   The feisty Scottish Terrier in that timeless Walt Disney film *Lady and the Tramp*.

JOPLIN   Janis, the sixties blues singer who was just as well known for her "sex, drugs and rock'n'roll" life-style. An outrageously raunchy name, so make sure your dog can live up to it.

JOSH   Shortened form of Joshua. *See* JESS

JUPITER   The largest of the planets in the solar sys-
            tem, Jupiter is a Latin word corresponding
            to the Sanskrit for "heavenly father." Jupiter
            was also the supreme deity of the ancient
            Romans.

K

KAREEM   Kareem Abdul-Jabbar, basketball great. A
            great name for the long, lean dog who
            invariably wins the game.

KATIE, KATY   An abbreviation of Katherine and the
            heroine of the celebrated children's novels
            by Susan Coolidge. For a small, cute dog.

KEEPER   Emily Brontë was a severe disciplinarian
            who frequently used the whip. Her Great
            Dane, Keeper, never left her side and was
            with her when she died.

KENNEDY   John Fitzgerald (1917-1963) the first Roman
            Catholic U.S. President, assassinated in

Dallas, Texas, supposedly by Lee Harvey
Oswald, in November 1963, after less than
three years in office.

KILLER   This name is not often bestowed seriously,
              but rather in jest. Perfect for the dog who
              leads burglars to the family silver and runs
              from the neighborhood cat.

KING   Among its other numerous applications, the
              King was the nickname of Clark Gable, the
              much adored film star. Perfect for the mutt
              that has a way with the ladies.

KING KONG   The monster-size gorilla in the 1933 film that made the Empire State Building look small. Use this name for a burly Boxer with brawn.

KOCH   For Ed Koch, ex-mayor of New York. For the dog who always seeks approval, and who always seems to be asking "How am I doing?"

L

LA FAYETTE   Marie Madeleine Pioche de la Vergne, Comtesse de La Fayette, wrote *La Princesse de Clèves* (1678), a novel about a woman whose marriage is shattered by a guilty passion. A great name for a dainty dog, with the diminutive, Faye.

LADON   While hunting with his hounds, Actaeon unwittingly intruded upon Diana bathing in a pool. The goddess changed him into a stag and he was torn to pieces by his own hounds, one of them Ladon. There must be a dog for whom this name would suitable.

LADY   This is number one on the "Guinness Book of Names" list of the most popular names for dogs in the United States. There are many reasons for this. There are *Lady and the Tramp*, Lady Day, lady-in-waiting, lady killer, Lady Luck, and, of course, Our Lady.

LAELAPS   This would be an excellent name for a gun dog. In the legend of Procris and Cephalus, Procris fled from Cephalus and was aided by the goddess Diana, who gave her a dog, Laelaps, who never failed to secure its prey.

LAIKA   The little Russian dog that became the first animal to be launched into orbit around the Earth during the space race between American and Russia in the late 50s and early 60s.

LALAGE   This is a name used in a poem by Horace for a young girl, presumably a chatterbox, as the word means "babbling." For the dog who barks incessantly.

LANCELOT   Sir Lancelot, Knight of the Round Table, and lover of King Arthur's wife Guinevere. For the dashing hound.

LASSIE   This name was made popular by a series of films about a Collie of exceptional qualities. Apparently the role was played by several different dogs, both male and female, over a period of two decades. *See* PAL

LAUREL and HARDY   Stanley Laurel and Oliver Hardy, an English and an American comedian, respectively, together made one of cinema's greatest comedy acts. They won an Oscar in 1932 for *The Music Box*.

LAZARUS   This mongrel mutt, owned by the eccentric Emperor Norton I of America, had the biggest funeral for a dog on record in 1862. It was held in San Francisco and about 10,000 people attended.

LEARY   Timothy Leary, the advocate of LSD. A name that would suit a dog who tunes out, turns over, and then drops off to sleep.

LEE   Robert E. Lee, Civil War general. A good name for a tenacious dog who's gallant and brave, even in the face of defeat.

LEO   The lion, from which names of heroes, saints and kings derive. The following lordly names originate from Leo: Leofric, Leofwin, Leon, Leonard, Leopold, Lionel and Lyall.

LIGHTNING   "Thunder is good, thunder is impressive; but it is the lightning that does the work," said Mark Twain. For the speedy hound with lots of energy.

LILINE   Liline was a favorite spaniel of Henry III of France, who had a superstitious faith in the judgement of these dogs. He once ignored her dislike of a visitor, Jacques Clement, who turned out to be his assassin.

LINCOLN   Abraham, President of the United States. For the dog adept at addressing crowds.

LLOYD   Lloyd George, Britain's Prime Minister in the First World War. A sombre name.

LOVELL/LOVEL   A name from the Middle Ages, best remembered by the famous lines nailed to the door of St. Paul's Cathedral, London, in 1484: "The cat, the rat, and Lovel our dog Rule all England under the hog."

LUATH   This was the name of the favorite dog of the Scottish poet Robert Burns. Irish mythology also has it that Luath was the name of a watchdog accidentally slain by the hero Cuchulain, who had to take the dog's place in penance.

LUCIA, LUCY   Names linked with virtuous persons, derived from "lux," the Latin for light, these would be suitable for gentle creatures of pedigreed stock. Other derivations include Lucian, Lucius, Lucas, Lucille, Lucilla and Luke.

LUCIFER   This name, with its dual connotations of good and evil, should not be a casual choice. Milton's Lucifer was princely. One can visualize a proud, elegant creature, a superb guard dog.

LUCKY   For that fortuitous dog that will charm the household.

LUDLAM   She was a sorceress with a reputedly lazy dog. The name suggests Luddite, so if you have the misfortune to own an idle scamp who is very destructive, this may be the name.

LUDWIG   Ludwig van Beethoven. For the dog who howls to "Moonlight Sonata."

LUPUS   Latin for "wolf."

LUTHER   Martin Luther (1483-1546), the German reformer, theologian and writer, mounted a lifelong struggle against the established Church, greatly influencing Christianity. For the dogmatic canine.

LYSANDER   In Shakespeare's *A Midsummer Night's Dream*, Lysander is the lover of Hermia, who has been ordered by her father to marry Demetrius, who in turn loves her friend Helena.

M

MADISON   James, fourth President of the United States (1809-1817). Another derivation could be the Madison dance.

MAFEKING   A regimental dog in the Boer War belonging to a detachment under the command of Baden-Powell. Mafeking briefly stopped the crossfire when he wandered out into the middle of the battlefield.

MAGGIO   Joe DiMaggio, the great American baseball player who was married briefly to Marilyn Monroe and who, allegedly, despised the decadence of Hollywood.

MAIDA   Another of Sir Walter Scott's dogs. *See* CAMP

MAJOR   Extremely popular, and quite fitting for an old, fuddy-duddy gundog.

MARMADUKE   If you have a big, clumsy and lovable Great Dane, then this name, from the famous cartoon strip "Marmaduke," will suit him down to the ground.

MARS   The red planet and Roman god. *See* DEIMOS

MARTHA   Paul McCartney of Beatles fame immortalized his dog Martha in a song he wrote about her.

MATHE   King Richard II's dog. When the King was deposed by Henry of Lancaster, Mathe, without a backward glance, switched his affections to the usurper. For the cur who bites the hand that feeds it.

MATILDA   Another name of Old German derivation, this one means "mighty battlemaid." It became popular in England after the Norman invasion, because it was the name of the wife of William the Conqueror. Tillie is a popular short form.

MAXIMILIAN   Means "greatest." Short form is Max. Usually given to dogs of the larger breeds,

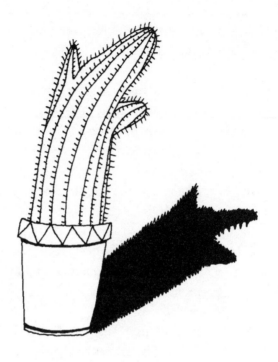

particularly German Shepherds, Doberman
Pinschers, Great Danes, Newfoundlands and
Old English Sheepdogs.

MELBA   A dog with some vocal ability would be
           required to fill the shoes of the famous
           opera singer, Dame Nellie Melba.

MELVILLE   Name your dog for Herman Melville,
           author of *Moby Dick*, and you may find
           that your pet has a taste for fish — with a
           vengeance.

MERLIN
The Prince of Enchanters. Son of a damsel seduced by a fiend, baptized and so rescued from the power of Satan. The name of the soothsayer of the King Arthur legend. For the dog with a touch of magic.

MICHAEL
This name provides many diminutives which are ideal names for dogs — Mike, Mick, Mickey, Mogga and Spike, the latter two being recent short forms. *See* SPIKE

MILLICENT
Again from the Old German, this name means "strong worker" or "energetic," and abbreviates to Millie. *See* MILLIE

MILLIE
White House resident and author of a best-selling autobiography. If your pet aspires to national office, here's a name for her.

MILTON
The great 17th-century poet and author of *Paradise Lost*, John Milton put religion back into Renaissance thought. A shortened form for a less highbrow canine could be Milt or even Miltie.

MING
Meaning "bright," this was the name adopted by the founder of the Chinese dynasty of the same name, from whence came the priceless Ming vases. For the decorative-looking dog.

MR. DOG   "A dog with money is addressed as Mr. Dog"— Spanish proverb.

MONGO   This comes from a Greek word meaning "hoarse" and was the nickname of Peter, Monophysite, Patriarch of Alexandria (c. 490 AD). A good name for a silent dog who wags its tail instead of barking for joy.

MONROE   Perfect for a dazzling dog or captivating canine. Name her for the one and only Marilyn. Alternatively, it's a good name for the fleabag with the *Seven Year Itch*.

MOOLAH   If your dog is consuming a large proportion of your income, or cost a lot to purchase, you could call it Moolah — slang for money.

MOOMIN   Perhaps your dog resembles the small, amiable hippo-like animals Tove Jansson created in the *Moomintrolls*, rather than a conventional canine. Moomintroll companions include Sniff, Snufkin, Groke, the Snork Maiden and the long-haired Muskrat.

MOPSER   "Has anybody seen my Mopser?
— A comely dog is he,
With hair the colour of Charles the Fifth,
And teeth like ships at sea."
— Walter de la Mare, *The Bandog*.

MORGAN   Full name: Morgan le Fay, fairy sister of
            King Arthur, "fae" being Old French for
            "fairy." For the dog who is light on its
            feet.

MUFFIN   This is a cuddly-sounding name loved by
            children, and it would suit a golden-brown-
            colored dog.

MURPHY   Murphy's law states that if anything can go
            wrong, it will. If your dog is suitably cynical,
            then this moniker would be appropriate. Be
            warned, though, that Murphy is also slang
            for a potato.

MUSKRAT   *See* MOOMIN

MUTTLEY   For a dog that giggles like Dick Dastardly's
            double-crossing sidekick in the TV cartoon
            "Wacky Races."

N

NANA   J.M. Barrie's name for the huge dog in *Peter
            Pan* who is loving nursemaid to the three

Darling children, Wendy, John and Michael.

NEAL   Cary Grant's dog in the film *Topper*. A good name for a large dog with a bit of a drinking problem.

NEHRU   Jawaharlal, the first Prime Minister of India, of great stature and eminence. For the independent dog.

NELSON   There have been many famous Nelsons throughout history, including Babyface (Charles) Nelson, the American gangster; Viscount Horatio Nelson, the English naval hero; and Nelson Mandela, the leader of the A.N.C.

NERO   After the Roman tyrant who fiddled while Rome burned. For the dog who watches burglars but doesn't stop them. *See* AHENOBARBUS

NEVILLE   Name your pet for Neville Chamberlain, the British Prime Minister, and you'll have a pet who'll always be willing to appease you.

NEWTON   After Sir Isaac. For the dog who realizes that what goes up must come down. *See* DIAMOND

"It's always 'Sit', 'Stay', 'Heel' — never 'Think', 'Innovate', 'Be yourself'".

Drawing by P. Steiner; © 1990 The New Yorker Magazine, Inc.

NICK   Nick Charles, the hero of the Thin Man
            films. A good name for a bloodhound or
            other tracking dog.

NIMBUS   A name which carries more romance than
            one initially imagines. The Oxford English
            Dictionary describes nimbus as "a bright
            cloud, or cloudlike splendour, imagined as
            investing deities when they appeared on
            earth." Does this sound like your dog?

NIPPER   If you think your dog appreciates good
            music, then name him after the small black-
            and-white dog who is pictured on RCA
            record labels listening to his master's
            voice.

NIXON   Republican President of the United States,
            disgraced over an election scandal. Never-
            theless, Nixon was one of the first Vice
            Presidents to take an active part in running
            the nation. A good name for an overkeen
            terrier. *See* CHECKERS

NODEL   *see* REYNARD

NOISETTE   This is a type of rose named for Philippe
            Noisette who first introduced it. It is a cross
            between a common China rose and a musk
            rose.

NORMAN   It is interesting to note that this name was quite common before the Norman Conquest, but died out in England during the Middle Ages. Norm and Normie, the common and affectionate diminutives, are perhaps less severe.

O

OBELIX   Asterix's partner in adventure, and the consumer of great quantities of wild boar. *See* ASTERIX, DOGMATIX

ODESSA   Name your dog for this Russian city, locale of Eisenstein's *Battleship Potemkin*, and you may find her a bit mutinous.

OLD YELLER   The family dog who contracts rabies and has to be shot in the Hollywood weepie of the same name.

OPIE   Opie Taylor, TV son of Andy Griffith. If your dog loves to accompany you on your fishing expeditions, here's a great name for him.

ORSON   Your pooch will be honored to be named for Orson Welles, the great actor and film-maker, but remember, Orson was rather portly...

OSCAR   Meaning "God-spear," Oscar is the name of many famous people: Oscar Hammerstein, Oscar Wilde, Oscar Niemeyer, and the film industry awards — the Oscars. Also suitable for a pair of total opposites, like Oscar and Felix in *The Odd Couple*.

OWENS   If your dog tends to take you for a walk, instead of the other way around, why not call him Owens, after the black American athlete Jesse Owens, who won four gold medals at the 1936 Olympic Games.

P

PADDINGTON   The only name for a dog from deepest, darkest Peru, found in a train station with a sign saying "Please look after this dog" around its neck. Must have a fondness for marmalade.

PAL   The first star of the Lassie films was, in fact, a laddie called Pal who lived a life of luxury during his film career. He was retired to a ranch after five years of making films, where he lived to the age of 19.

PANDY   In Dodie Smith's *101 Dalmatians*, Pandy is the smallest and youngest of the ill-fated litter of pups which falls into Cruella de Ville's evil hands.

PASHA   An attractive name, which is actually the
           title in Turkey of officers of high rank in
           military or civic positions. For the dignified
           dog.

PAVLOV   The perfect name for the dog whose breed
           is noted for its excessive drooling, or for the
           dog who always knows when it's time for
           dinner.

PEGASUS   The winged horse on whose back
           Bellerophon rode against the mythical
           monster, the Chimera. Would suit a dog
           with stature, like a Great Dane or a
           Doberman.

PENN   William Penn, Quaker leader, or Sean Penn,
           "Brat Pack" member. For dogs with a range
           of temperament.

PERCY   *see* DUDLEY

PERDY   Devoted partner to Pongo and mother of his
           pups in *101 Dalmatians*.

PERI   A fairy-like or elfin being in Persian mythol-
           ogy.

PERITES   Alexander the Great's favorite canine was
           the last of an illustrious breed of dog and

could slay a lion in a matter of minutes. An ideal name for a guard dog.

PETER   Peter the Great established Russia as northern Europe's leading military power. If, much to your relief, your hound is not in the least bit warlike, then name him after St. Peter, who was devoted to Jesus.

PETIE   The dog from "The Little Rascals". Many a pup's a little rascal — here's a name for your little one.

PHOBOS   *see* DEIMOS

PICASSO   For the dog who has his blue periods, but also his pink periods, and if your canine resembles a cube, all the better.

PICKLES   The terrier shopkeeper in Beatrix Potter's *Ginger and Pickles*. Ginger is a yellow cat.

PINSCHER   A Doberman, of course.

PLUTO   A very popular name for black dogs. In mythology, Pluto was god of his own dark realm, the entrance to which was guarded by a huge three-headed dog, Cerberus. Also the name of a popular Walt Disney dog.

PONGO   In *101 Dalmatians* by Dodie Smith, Pongo is the father of the stolen litter of puppies. *See* PERDY

PRINCE   There's a Prince for almost every breed — Prince of Darkness (Satan); Prince of Peace (Christ); Prince of Wales (Charles); Prince of Humbug (Phineas T. Barnum, the circus owner); Prince of Destruction (Timur the Lame, the Mongol conqueror renowned for his cruelty); Prince of Artists (Albrecht Dürer, the great German artist). And the list goes on. *See* GOLDIE

PUCCINI   The Italian composer of such great operas as *Madame Butterfly* and *La Bohème*. The

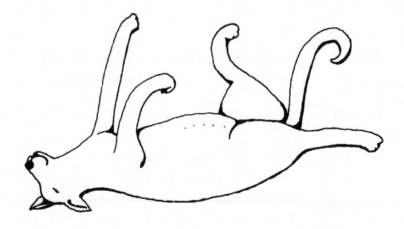

perfect name for the favorite pet of a musical family.

PUMPKIN   For a beast acquired at Halloween or on Thanksgiving Day. The name is used by some as a term of endearment. Could denote an orange-brown color.

PUNCH   That violent puppet who bludgeons his wife Judy to death. Or the equally outrageous satirical English magazine. Not for a meek and mild mutt.

Q

QADDAFI   Name your dog for the Libyan leader, and you may be asking for trouble. However, if your dog leads his friends on rampages through the neighborhood, this might be a good name for him.

QUAYLE   A great name for a handsome, but not very bright canine.

QUEENIE   *see* DUCHESS

QUINCY   If your dog has an ear for music, why not
            name him after Quincy Jones, famous record
            producer for Michael Jackson, Tina Turner,
            and Liza Minelli, to name a few.

R

RAFFLES   Sir Thomas Stamford Bingley Raffles (1781-
            1826), British founder of Singapore. Also
            the gentleman burglar and cricketer in
            novels by E.W. Hornung. An apt name for a
            risk-taker, with connotations of lottery and
            gambling, derived from a game of chance of
            that name.

RALPH   This means "counsel-wolf," and is both an
            Old Norse and Anglo-Saxon name. It's the
            sort of name that suits the feistier, less
            sensitive breeds of dog.

RAMEKIN   Or Ramequin. Sounds like a fabulous fic-
            tional name. Use it for that fairy-tale dog,
            though remember that, literally, it applies to
            something small. Wonderful for a Bichon
            Frise.

RANDOLPH — This abbreviates to Randy, a popular name in America for audacious mutts. It is more popular in England in its longer form, being a family name of the Marlboroughs.

RASPUTIN — The Russian monk and mystic, known for his drunkenness, sexual excess and nepotism. An enigmatic, exotic name, but use it cautiously as it may have arcane powers.

REAGAN — After Ronald, former U.S. President. The perfect name for the dog who yearns for a bigger backyard.

REMUS — *see* ROMULUS

REVERE — Paul Revere's midnight ride is one of America's most inspiring events. If your dog is the world's best watchdog, or if he wakes you up in the middle of the night...

REYNARD — The beast-epic poem, *Roman de Renart*, of the 14th century, is a satire on the state of Germany in the Middle Ages, with the church represented by Reynard the fox, the baronial classes represented by the wolf Isengrin, and royalty by Nodel the lion.

RILEY — There are times when a person feels that his dog has a more comfortable and jolly life than he does — in fact, "a life of Riley." A good name for a much-loved family pet.

RIN TIN TIN   Canine hero of film fame. What dog wouldn't be flattered to be named after one of the world's great movie stars?

ROCKEFELLER   A good name for the dog who has everything, or for the philanthropic dog, or perhaps for the dog with a taste for oysters.

ROGER   Yet another war-derived name, this one comes from Anglo-Saxon words meaning "fame" and "spear," and was a very popular name from the time of the Domesday Book until the 16th century.

ROMULUS and REMUS   The twin sons of Mars and Rhea Silvia, who were suckled by a she-wolf after their mother was slain. They began building Rome but argued, and Romulus killed his brother. Perfect for canine sibling rivals.

ROOSEVELT   F.D.R. was a great dog-lover. His little dog, Fala, was his longtime companion. Teddy Roosevelt was known as "Rough and Ready." Name your dog for either man, and your pet will surely live up to a noble name.

RORY   With clearly rolled r's, this is a grand name for a dog of an Irish or a Scottish breed.

ROSE   "What's in a name?
That which we call a rose
By any other name would smell as sweet."

ROVER   A bit common. Do not expect this pooch to be home in time for dinner. A wandering cur with a definite wild streak, a bit of a cad and highly unreliable.

RUBENS   Sir Peter Paul, the prolific Flemish painter, famous for his fleshy women. A wonderful name for the female with a "Renaissance" figure who is colorful, exotic and sensual, like the paintings.

RUBY   In the 19th century, jewel names became popular, and the name Ruby was among them. The first recorded use of the name is in "John Peel," the old English hunting song, in which one of the hounds is called Ruby.

RUDOLPH   Only to be used if the mutt comes into your life at Christmas, or if he really does have a red nose, like the famed reindeer. The abbreviation Rudy has long been popular in the United States.

RUFUS   This name is of Latin derivation, meaning
             red or reddish. It has been bestowed as a
             nickname upon many famous people, includ-
             ing William II of England in reference to
             his ruddy complexion.

RUSSELL   For a Jack Russell Terrier.

RUSTY   When the color of your dog is a pretty
             indiscriminate mix of red and brown, then
             no other name will do but Rusty.

S

SACHA, SASHA   An elegant name for male or female,
             Sacha is short for Alexander. Suitable for a
             Borzoi or an Afghan hound.

SADDAM   A good name for a tyrannical dog. Does
             your pet overrun and ruin the neighbor's
             garden? Does he loot the neighbor dog's
             bone cache?

SALLY   This name is suitable for a small female dog
             with a twinkle in her eye and a bounce to

her step, but will not do for a larger dog with family responsibilities.

SALOMÉ   You will know at once whether your bitch is a Salomé, a sinuous, hypnotic name. It would suit a Greyhound or any slender female with the right qualities.

SAMSON   Dogs are intuitive, and the name will suggest to him all your expectations. This is not suitable for a breed which is traditionally close-shorn.

SAMUEL/SAM   From the Hebrew, meaning "heard by God." The shortening, Sam, became popular in America after the invention of Uncle Sam. Ideal for the patriotic canine.

SANDY   If it is made clear that the dog's name is Alexander, you may suffer no embarrassment; after all, the kids chose it. It should bear some relation to the dog's coloring.

SARAH   For Sarah Bernhardt, the French tragedienne who played both male and female roles and who came to be known as the Divine Sarah.

SCOOBY DOO   The lovable cartoon dog without a scrap of courage that loves to eat when he's

scared. For the type of dog who would lead burglars to the family silver.

SCRAPPY DOO   The young nephew of Scooby Doo who has too much bravado. Faces dangerous situations with a war cry of "Puppy Power!" A good name for a fearless pup.

SCRUB   This and Scruffy are used as dog's names from time to time, but they are not recommended. One should expect more from one's pets, and the best names enhance.

SHANE   The right name for an Irish Setter, but it has been known as the name for a Dachshund. Whatever the breed, you'll never be ashamed of choosing Shane.

SHARP   This was the name of Queen Victoria's Rough Collie. He can be seen in several royal portraits, and in one he is seated by the throne. This is strictly a name for regal breeds.

SHEBA   Queen of Arabia renowned for her beauty and wealth. Today the title is used for someone who gives herself airs and graces. If your exotic dog has got it all, encourage the bitch to flaunt it with this imperial name.

SIEGFRIED This name, associated more often these days with the popular TV show "All Creatures Great and Small" than with grand opera, could be used for most dogs, although it would be more common among those of German extraction. Highly recommended.

SIRIUS Sirius is not often used as a dog's name, but it should be, because Sirius is the dog star and the brightest in the night sky.

SKIP/SKIPPY Only for a very bouncy dog, after Australia's most famous bush kangaroo, star of the "Skippy" TV series, rumored to be making a comeback in a new, environmentally aware show.

SKIPPER A very jolly name, though sea dogs are rare. There are two indications: he may be the leader of the litter or just a lively little chap, however remarkable the mixture.

SLY Sylvester "Sly" Stallone. For the very muscular breeds or for any dog born in Philadelphia. Or use it more literally if he's sly or crafty.

SNAP This is obviously short and snappy, and there the danger lies. So long as he is kept on a leash there should be no trouble.

SNOOPY   The lovable beagle created by Charles M.
           Schulz in the "Peanuts" comic strips. If your
           dog tends to sleep on top of his doghouse or
           pretends to be the Red Baron or Joe Cool,
           this is the perfect name.

SOFTIE   If you've searched the length and breadth of
           this book and still can't find a name that
           suits your family pet, then this is a last
           resort.

Drawing by John O'Brien; © 1990 The New Yorker Magazine, Inc.

SOOTY   Together with Snowflake, Smuts and Snow-
           ball, this name suggests color-consciousness.
           They either state the obvious or are used in
           jest — for example, naming a black kitten
           Snowflake.

SPAM   The much maligned luncheon meat. A
           good, fun name for a mutt of indefinable
           breeding.

SPIKE   A name growing in popularity. It calls to
           mind Spike Milligan, the famous Goon, an
           animal lover and activist. You will know a
           Spike when you see one.

SPORT   An affectionate nickname, appropriate for a
           gamester.

SPOT   Not a name for the discerning, however
           obvious the spot may be, although fans
           of Eric Hill's well-loved children's book
           and television character may feel differently.
           It would probably do very well for a
           mongrel with a spot, owned by a family with
           children.

SPRAT   "Jack Sprat could eat no fat…" Perfect for
           the lean or fussy hound who may or may not
           be partnered with a female who can eat no
           lean.

STANLEY   Kubrick, legendary American film director responsible for such films as *Lolita*, *A Clockwork Orange*, and more recently, *Full Metal Jacket*. A name only for a very unusual and extraordinary dog.

STAR   If your dog moves like a meteor, fights like Mars, and eats like a black hole, yet is the light of your life, perhaps this is just the name.

STELLA   Stella is Latin for "star," and was first coined as a name by Sir Philip Sidney. His collection of sonnets and songs named *Astrophel and Stella* (c. 1582) was written for Lady Penelope Devereux, whom he was wooing.

SULTAN   This is a noble, kingly name; one envisages a large, sleek, black creature, perfectly trained.

SUSIE   Like Sally, this name is without distinction, despite the suggestion of amiability and sunshine. Would be quite suitable for a small unpretentious Cairn.

SWIFT   After the English satirist, Jonathan Swift. Also rapid or fast, for the speedy breeds such as Greyhounds and Whippets.

T

TAFF/TAFFY   A familiar form of address or nickname for a Welshman, derived from the Welsh pronunciation of Davy or David. Taffy can mean blarney, sweet-talking or coarse flattery.

TAGGY, TALGERT   Derived from Agnes, as is Annis. Very pleasing names for short and friendly breeds.

TALBOT   The Talbot hound is a now-extinct breed of hound used for tracking in the 16th century, a large pale-colored dog with long hanging ears and great powers of smell. Chaucer used this as a dog's name.

TANGO   The code word to represent the letter "T," a seductive Argentine ballroom dance or its music, or for the film *The Last Tango in Paris*; this is a versatile name.

TARQUIN   When Tarquinius Sextus raped Lucretia, the Tarquins were expelled from Rome and the Republic set up in their place. Be warned: your pooch could become a blackguardly cur under the influence of this name.

TENNESSEE   In the prologue to *Camino Real*, American playwright Tennessee Williams wrote
"It is a terrible thing for an old woman to
outlive her dogs." Still, a good name for the
dog with dramatic flair.

TEX or TEXAN   For the lone-star dog with a real
Southern drool who likes to roll around in
oil.

THATCHER   For the "iron lady" of the canine world.

THISBE   This amusing, gay little name brings to
mind the workmen's play in *A Midsummer
Night's Dream*. It was also the name of Marie
Antoinette's Toy Spaniel, given to her by
way of apology by Louis XVI (who killed
her own little dog in a fit of rage).

TIGE   Buster Brown's companion. Both live inside
a shoe. Good name for a pup who's fond of
footwear.

TINY   Another name used best ironically.

TITUS   Titus (c. AD 39-81) was a Roman emperor
who put an end to treason trials and drove
out informers. Almost all hostilities ceased
during his reign. For a dog who longs for
the peaceful life.

TOBY   From the Hebrew "Tobias," this means "the Lord is good." Punch's dog (in "Punch and Judy") bears the name.

TOLSTOY   After Leo, author of *War and Peace* — an appropriate description of life in many households.

TOSCA   An opera by Puccini. Beware of an inclination towards the tragic. Masculine is Tosco, but the feminine sounds better.

TOTO   Dorothy's beloved little dog in *The Wizard of Oz*.

TOWSER   A name first used in the 17th century for a large dog, particularly those used to bait bears or bulls. Only for those owners fond of blood sports.

TRIXIE   This is the short form of Beatrice, and quite a common name for dainty little dogs.

TROTSKY   Leon Trotsky, Stalin's nemesis, exiled from Russia in 1929 and assassinated in Mexico in 1940. For a Chihuahua, or for any dog who likes a good run in the morning.

TRUFFE   Childhood pet of Alexandre Dumas, author of *The Three Musketeers*. The dog was obviously of massive proportions, as Dumas remembered riding on its back.

TRUMAN   Harry S, U.S. President, famous for accepting ultimate responsibility for U.S. actions. "The buck stops here" was his favorite motto. For the pooch who confesses his mistakes.

TRUMPER   Trumpery is fraud, imposture or trickery. A good name for the mutt who continually hoodwinks you.

TRUSTY   Perhaps after the bloodhound in Walt Disney's *Lady and the Tramp*, but this is a risky name to give a young dog unless you are happy with irony.

V

VALENTINE   This would be a perfect name for a gift of love, after St. Valentine's Day, the 14th of February, the day of lovers, which is named for a Christian martyred in Rome (c. 270).

VERNE   For Jules Verne, the great science fiction writer. For the dog who sometimes makes you wish you could send him to the moon.

VESPUCCI   (Spelled Vespoochi?) After Amerigo Vespucci, the Italian navigator.

VICTOR   This name needs no explanation, having been adopted into English directly from the Latin. It would suit those breeds known for their ability to win the fight — Rottweilers and Bull Terriers come quickly to mind.

VIGI   Vigi was a large, shaggy, iron-grey hound from Gaelic legend who was adopted by Olaf I, King of the Vikings, for his cleverness and speed.

VINCENT   Van Gogh (1853-90). A Dutch painter much influenced by Impressionism. His work has recently sold for record prices, but his image in the popular mind is much influenced by his mental instability. Appropriate for a dog with one ear.

VIRGIL   (70-19 BC) Roman poet. Virgil's *Georgics* (36-29 BC) is a four-volume agricultural treatise, written with characteristic pathos and love, reporting careful observation of animals and nature. *See* GEORGE

VIVA   A shout or exclamation from the Italian, meaning "Long live!" A great, exuberant name to call out loud.

VIXEN   This name has a great ring to it. It is the name for a female fox, or traditionally means a shrewish or quarrelsome woman. For the fiery redhead.

VLADIMIR Vladimir I (956-1015) was a Ukrainian-Scandinavian saint. Once an unruly Viking,

he converted to Christianity and married, then brought his religion to his subjects. For the born-again mutt.

W

WALDO   A name that recalls that old scamp in *Under Milk Wood* by Dylan Thomas. The name originates from the Old English Waltheof, a compound of "power," "rule," and, unfortunately, "thief."

WAMBA   In Sir Walter Scott's *Ivanhoe* (1820), the jester of Cedric the Saxon. For the dog whose antics make you laugh, and whose devotion warms your heart.

WASHINGTON   Good name for a dog of American descent, even though this name originates from the English village Wassa and actually means "home of the people of Wassa."

WATSON   Dr. Watson, Sherlock Holmes's partner. A good name for a smart dog who's always overshadowed by true genius.

WAYNE   Name your high-pitched dog for Wayne
         Newton, or perhaps for "Mad" Anthony
         Wayne, hero of the American Revolution.

WESLEY   Like DUDLEY, this name was originally a
         surname.

WILBUR   Another name from the Old German, this
         one means "will" and "defense." Wilbur was
         the name of one of the Wright brothers, the
         aviation pioneers.

WILLIAM Wills is the obvious diminutive if your dog
         is a little prince.

WINDSOR Popular with British royalty, the Corgi was
         introduced to Queen Elizabeth II by her
         father when he was Duke of York. Rozavel
         Golden Eagle, better known as Dookie, was
         their first dog.

WINSTON This name derives from a hamlet in
         Gloucestershire of the same name. It is also
         associated with British Prime Minister Sir
         Winston Churchill. His resemblance to
         little babies and Boxer dogs has resulted in
         many small creatures bearing the name.

WODEHOUSE   Pelham Grenville Wodehouse (1881-
         1975) wrote over 120 volumes and created

well-loved characters including Jeeves, the wise and resourceful valet, and his amiable but vacuous employer, Bertie Wooster.

WOLF   *see* GOLDIE

WOODHOUSE   The English dog trainer Barbara Woodhouse is claimed in the *Guinness Book of Records* to have been the most successful trainer of dogs. A good name for those dogs who need constant reminders of obedience.

WOODRUFF   A woodland herb found in Britain and Europe; it has small white flowers and

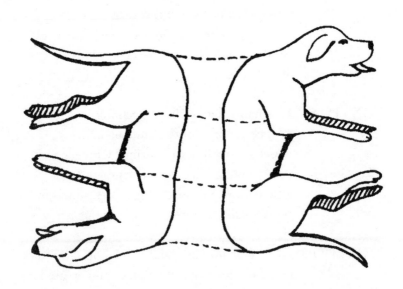

strongly scented leaves. For those with a strong doggy smell.

Y

YAHOO — A brute with human form and rough and uncouth manner, from Swift's *Gulliver's Travels*.

YALE — Name your dog for this Ivy League college, or perhaps after the lock manufacturer. A good name for the studious pup, or for one devoted to keeping his owner secure.

YASSIR — Arafat, if he's a bit of a terror.

YOGI — For Yogi Bear, the bumbling bruin of Jellystone Park. *See* BOO BOO

YORICK — For the jester who's always digging up bones.

YUPPIE — For the Young Urban Pet with the most up-to-date accessories. For your yuppie puppie.

YURI   Yuri Gagarin, the first man in space. Laika, the first dog in space, preceded him.

Z

ZAPPA   Frank Zappa, avant-garde musician. Zappa named his children Dweezil and Moon Unit, so don't hesitate to name your dog for him — he won't be offended.

ZARA   Marasquin de Zara is a renowned liqueur made at Zara, a Dalmatian village situated on the Adriatic. The liqueur is much used in pastry and confectionery. Sounds like a dog's name.

ZENGER American journalist whose trial established the tradition of the freedom of the press in the British colonies. Perfect name for the dog fond of newsprint.

ZEPPO   One of the Marx Brothers. *See* GROUCHO

ZESTE   From French for "peel"; it means something which gives relish or flavor. An appropriate

name for an important addition to the
family, particularly one with strong inclina-
tions and gusto.

ZETA The sixth letter of the Greek alphabet, and
it has a great sound to it. This name could
be useful if the number six is significant.
Perhaps you could call your sixth dog this.

ZIEGFELD Flo Ziegfeld, theatrical producer. If every
walk with your pooch requires elaborate
preparation.

ZINGANO/ZINGARO This name means "gypsy" in
Italian, and is a suitable name for an under-
dog in most parts of the world.

ZIP A speedy dog who sets the pace for the
morning jog.

ZOE This is the Greek version of the name Eve,
meaning "life." It was a popular name in the
Roman Empire, and then in England after
about 1850, and most recently in the
United States.

ZOILUS Or, in Greek, Zoilos. He was a shrewd,
witty and harsh critic of Homer, Plato and
Isocrates. He was nicknamed "Homer's
scourge" for his assault on the *Odyssey*.

ZORBA   Can your dog dance? Then name him after
             the hero of the movie *Zorba the Greek*.

Index